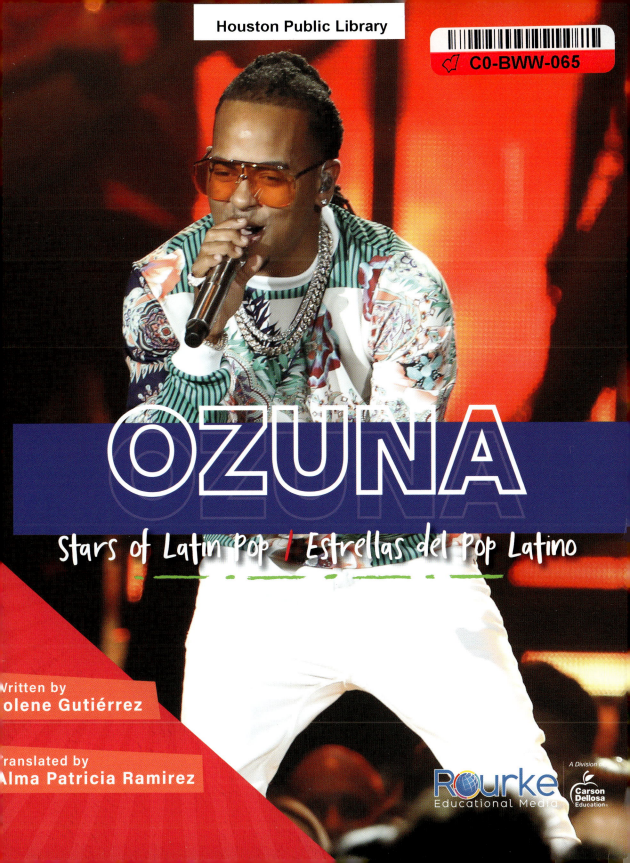

OZUNA

Stars of Latin Pop / Estrellas del Pop Latino

Written by
Jolene Gutiérrez

Translated by
Alma Patricia Ramirez

Rourke
Educational Media

A Division of
Carson Dellosa
Education

Before Reading: *Building Background Knowledge and Vocabulary*

Building background knowledge can help children process new information and build upon what they already know. Before reading a book, it is important to tap into what children already know about the topic. This will help them develop their vocabulary and increase their reading comprehension.

Questions and Activities to Build Background Knowledge:

1. Look at the front cover of the book and read the title. What do you think this book will be about?
2. What do you already know about this topic?
3. Take a book walk and skim the pages. Look at the table of contents, photographs, captions, and bold words. Did these text features give you any information or predictions about what you will read in this book?

Vocabulary: *Vocabulary Is Key to Reading Comprehension*

Use the following directions to prompt a conversation about each word.
- Read the vocabulary words.
- What comes to mind when you see each word?
- What do you think each word means?

Vocabulary Words:		Palabras del vocabulario	
• collaborated	• microphone	• collaboró	• micrófono
• crossover	• paternal	• debut	• paterna
• debut	• reggaetón	• fusión	• reguetón

During Reading: *Reading for Meaning and Understanding*

To achieve deep comprehension of a book, children are encouraged to use close reading strategies. During reading, it is important to have children stop and make connections. These connections result in deeper analysis and understanding of a book.

 ## Close Reading a Text

During reading, have children stop and talk about the following:
- Any confusing parts
- Any unknown words
- Text to text, text to self, text to world connections
- The main idea in each chapter or heading

Encourage children to use context clues to determine the meaning of any unknown words. These strategies will help children learn to analyze the text more thoroughly as they read.

When you are finished reading this book, turn to the next-to-last page for **After Reading Questions** and an **Activity**.

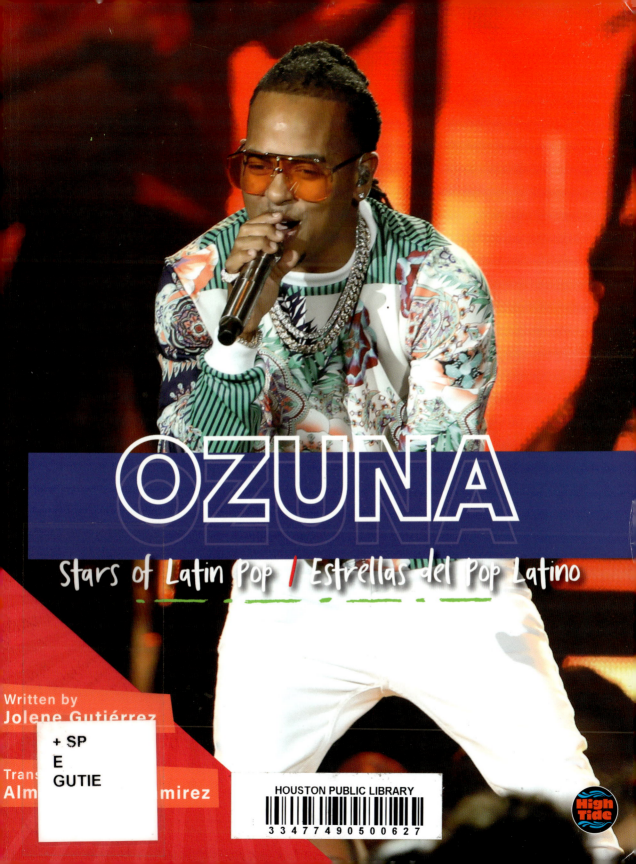

OZUNA

Stars of Latin Pop / Estrellas del Pop Latino

Written by
Jolene Gutiérrez

Trans...
Alm...   ...mirez

High Tide

Table of Contents

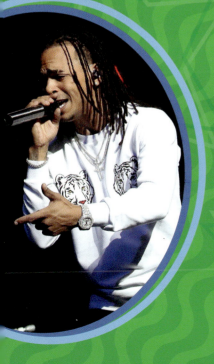

Tabla de contenido

Microphones and Music

Micrófonos y música

Juan Carlos Ozuna Rosado was born in San Juan, Puerto Rico. Juan's father was a dancer who died when Juan was just three years old. Juan's mother was involved in his life, but Juan was raised mostly by his **paternal** grandmother Eneida.

• • •

Juan Carlos Ozuna Rosado nació en San Juan, Puerto Rico. El padre de Juan fue un bailarín que murió cuando Juan tenía solo tres años. La madre de Juan estuvo involucrada en su vida, pero Juan creció la mayor parte del tiempo con su abuela **paterna** Eneida.

paternal (puh-TUR-nuhl): being related to someone through your father

paterna (pa-ter-na): relacionado con alguien por parte de padre

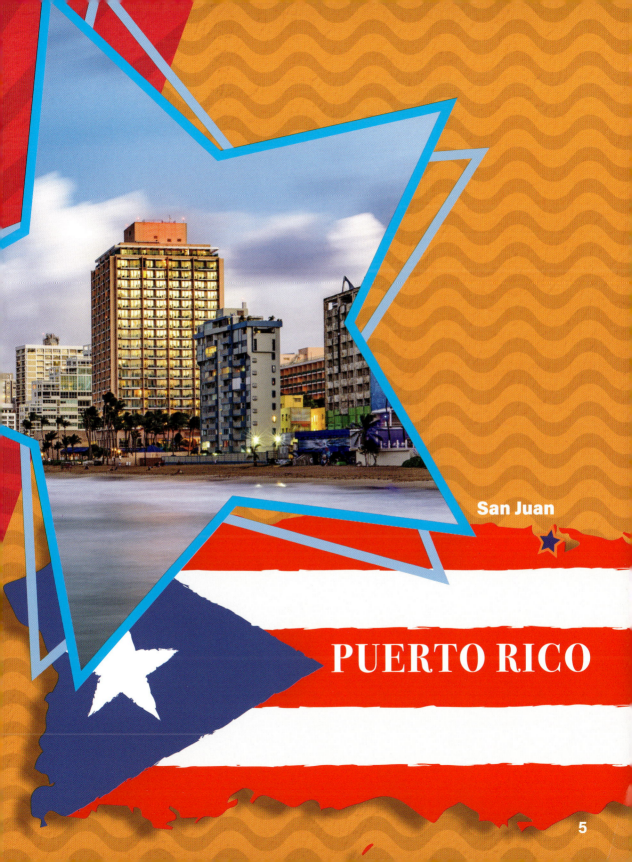

San Juan

PUERTO RICO

Juan's uncle Felix became a father figure. He gave Juan his first **microphone** when Juan was 12 years old. Juan started to write songs and perform in public. Felix would play music, and Juan would sing. Felix said Juan would always know all the songs. Later, Juan would say, "It's in my blood to work in music."

• • •

Félix, el tío de Juan, se convirtió en una figura paterna. Le dio a Juan su primer **micrófono** cuando Juan tenía 12 años. Juan comenzó a escribir canciones y a presentarse en público. Félix tocaba la música y Juan cantaba. Félix dijo que Juan siempre se sabía todas las canciones. Luego, Juan decía: "El trabajo con la música lo llevo en la sangre".

microphone (MYE-kruh-fone): an instrument used to amplify sounds or to record sounds

micrófono (mi-cró-fo-no): un instrumento que se usa para amplificar los sonidos o para grabar los sonidos

Ozuna's Odyssey
La odisea de Ozuna

When Juan was singing, he called himself J Oz. Later, he changed his stage name to his father's last name, Ozuna. Ozuna mostly performs **reggaetón** and rap.

• • •

Cuando Juan estaba cantando, se autonombró J Oz. Después, cambió su nombre artístico al apellido de su padre, Ozuna. Ozuna canta principalmente **reguetón** y rap.

reggaetón (reg-ay-TONE): music influenced by Jamaican music, includes singing and rapping, usually in Spanish

reguetón (re-gue-tón): música influenciada por la música de Jamaica, incluye cantar y rapear, generalmente en español

In 2010, Ozuna moved to New York City, New York. While in New York, he created his first music video for less than $100. In 2014, Ozuna moved back to Puerto Rico and started posting his music on YouTube. He has tried "from day one, writing songs people could identify with."

• • •

En 2010, Ozuna se fue a vivir a la ciudad de Nueva York, Nueva York. Mientras estaba en Nueva York, creó su primer video musical que le costó menos de $100. En 2014, Ozuna regresó a Puerto Rico y comenzó a publicar su música en YouTube. Él ha tratado "desde el primer día, de escribir canciones con las que las personas se puedan identificar".

Ozuna's Oso

Oso was inspired by a teddy bear that Ozuna's daughter gave him. He is Ozuna's mascot and logo and has been in many of his music videos. Oso also appears on Ozuna's apparel and merchandise. Ozuna even wears him on a necklace!

• • •

Oso de Ozuna

Oso se inspiró en un oso de peluche que la hija de Ozuna le regaló. Es la mascota y logotipo de Ozuna y ha aparecido en muchos de sus videos musicales. Oso también aparece en la ropa y mercancía de Ozuna. ¡Ozuna incluso lo usa en un collar!

In 2015, Ozuna performed more than 300 shows in Puerto Rico. "I never imagined my career would take off this fast." In 2017, Ozuna's first studio album came out. The album was called *Odisea* and reached multi-platinum status.

• • •

En 2015, Ozuna se presentó en más de 300 espectáculos en Puerto Rico. "Nunca imaginé que mi carrera despegara tan rápido". En 2017, salió el primer álbum de estudio de Ozuna. El álbum se llamó *Odisea* y alcanzó el estatus multiplatino.

The Path to Platinum

Ozuna is on an odyssey, or journey, to the top! In the United States, an album has to sell at least one million copies to reach platinum status. This number may differ in other countries because of their population.

● ● ●

El camino hacia el platino

¡Ozuna está en una odisea, o viaje, hacia la cima! En Estados Unidos, un álbum tiene que vender al menos un millón de copias para alcanzar el estatus de platino. Este número puede ser diferente en otros países debido a su población.

13

Ozuna won eleven awards at the 2018 Billboard Music Awards, including Top Latin Album and Top Latin Artist. That is the most awards ever won by an artist at the Billboard Latin Music Awards.

• • •

Ozuna ganó once premios en los Billboard Music Awards de 2018, incluido el Top Latin Album y el Top Latin Artist. Es el artista que más premios ha ganado en el Billboard Latin Music Awards.

Watch This!

Ozuna loves collecting watches! His grandmother gave him a *Toy Story* watch when he was young. Now, he has a collection of watches. His favorite is a NASCAR racing watch.

• • •

¡Mira!

¡A Ozuna le gusta coleccionar relojes! Su abuela le dio un reloj de *Toy Story* cuando era joven. Ahora, él tiene una colección de relojes. Su favorito es un reloj de carreras de NASCAR.

Some people call Ozuna the new king of reggaetón. Ozuna says, "I'm doing music for my people; I work for my people. I'm doing this because I love it."

• • •

Algunas personas llaman a Ozuna el nuevo rey del reguetón. Ozuna dice: "Estoy haciendo música para mi gente, trabajo para mi gente. Lo hago porque me gusta".

Thankful for Thanksgiving Parade

In 2019, Ozuna was in New York City's Macy's Thanksgiving Day Parade. He said he has seen it on TV for years, and it was like a dream to ride a float and sing in the parade.

● ● ●

Agradecido por el desfile del Día de Acción de Gracias

En 2019, Ozuna participó en el desfile del Día de Acción de Gracias de Macy's en la ciudad de Nueva York. Dijo que lo había visto en la televisión durante años y que era como un sueño subirse a un carro alegórico y cantar en el desfile.

Ozuna has worked with other famous artists! He's **collaborated** with Snoop Dogg, Daddy Yankee, Selena Gomez, and J Balvín. He also persuaded Cardi B to sing in Spanish.

● ● ●

¡Ozuna ha trabajado con otros artistas famosos! Él **colaboró** con Snoop Dogg, Daddy Yankee, Selena Gomez y J Balvín. También convenció a Cardi B para que cantara en español.

collaborated (kuh-LAB-uh-rate-ed): worked together to accomplish or achieve something

colaboró (co-la-bo-ró): trabajaron juntos para lograr o alcanzar algo

Ozuna performs with Cardi B.
Ozuna se presentó con Cardi B.

Ozuna is practicing English, too. He travels with someone who only speaks English so he can learn the language. Ozuna says, "I want to go for the crossover."

• • •

Ozuna también está practicando el inglés. Viaja con alguien que solo habla inglés para que pueda aprender el idioma. Ozuna dice: "Quiero lograr la fusión".

crossover (KRAWS-oh-ver): music or musicians liked by different audiences; often winning awards or being listed on two different record charts

fusión (fu-sión): música o músicos que les gustan a diferentes audiencias, a menudo ganan premios o aparecen en diferentes listas de discos

His popularity is growing! In 2019, Ozuna made his acting **debut** in a movie, *Qué León*. He was named one of *Time* magazine's 100 Most Influential People in the world. He won four Guinness Records in 2019, including most-watched artist on YouTube.

● ● ●

¡Su popularidad está creciendo! En 2019, Ozuna hizo su **debut** como actor en la película, *Qué León*. La revista *Time* lo nombró entre las 100 personas con más influencia en el mundo. El ganó cuatro récords de Guines en 2019, incluido el artista con más visitas en YouTube.

debut (day-BYOO): doing something for the first time, usually referring to something artistic

debut (de-but): hacer algo por primera vez, normalmente se refiere a algo artístico

Odyssey Children's Charity

La Fundación Odisea Children

In 2017, after the success of his first album, Ozuna created a charity. He called the charity Odyssey Children, and it was created to help children in Puerto Rico.

• • •

En 2017, después del éxito de su primer álbum, Ozuna creó una fundación de caridad. Él llamó a la fundación de caridad Odisea Children, y fue creada para ayudar a los niños en Puerto Rico.

After Hurricane Maria hit Puerto Rico, Ozuna's charity became even more important. Odyssey Children provides clothing, hot meals, and even gifts to those in need. Ozuna gives part of his monthly earnings to his foundation to help as many people as he can. He says, "It comes from my heart."

• • •

Después de que el huracán María azotó a Puerto Rico, la fundación de caridad de Ozuna se volvió aún más importante. La fundación Odisea Children proporciona ropa, comida caliente e incluso regalos para aquellos que lo necesitan. Ozuna entrega parte de sus ganancias mensuales a su fundación para ayudar a tantas personas como se pueda. Él dice: "Me sale del corazón".

A Devastating Storm

Hurricane Maria was a Category 5 storm, the strongest type of hurricane. September 16 through September 30, 2017, the storm struck the islands of Dominica, St. Croix, and Puerto Rico. This hurricane caused hundreds of deaths and severe damage to the islands.

• • •

Una tormenta devastadora

El huracán María fue una tormenta de categoría 5, el tipo de huracán más fuerte. Del 16 de septiembre al 30 de septiembre de 2017, la tormenta golpeó las islas de Dominica, St. Croix y Puerto Rico. Este huracán ocasionó cientos de muertes y daños severos a las islas.

27

Ozuna has advice to share, too. He works hard to be successful. He reminds others to do the same. Ozuna says: "Things aren't gifted to you. Things don't just come from an idea, from nothing. You have to work for them. You have to pursue them. You have to take time. You have to sacrifice."

• • •

Ozuna también tiene consejos para compartir. Trabaja duro para tener éxito. Les recuerda a los demás que hagan lo mismo. Ozuna dice: "Las cosas no te las regalan. Las cosas no surgen simplemente de una idea, de la nada. Tienes que trabajar para conseguirlas. Tienes que perseguirlas. Tienes que tomarte un tiempo. Tienes que sacrificarte."

Index

After Reading Questions

1. How was Ozuna's family important to his success?

2. Why do you think Ozuna changed his stage name from J Oz to Ozuna?

3. Why do you think learning English is important to Ozuna?

4. What are some of the awards Ozuna has earned?

5. What is Ozuna doing to help children?

Activity

Ozuna started a watch collection because he received a watch as a gift from his grandmother. Do you have any collections? If so, what are they? If not, what would you like to collect? Draw or write about the items that are or would be in your collection. How many would you like to have? What is your favorite part of your collection? How will you take care of your collection and keep it safe? Will you share your collection with others?

Índice

Preguntas para después de la lecturas

1. ¿Qué importancia tuvo la familia de Ozuna en su éxito?

2. ¿Por qué crees que Ozuna cambió su nombre artístico de J Oz a Ozuna?

3. ¿Por qué crees que aprender inglés es importante para Ozuna?

4. ¿Cuáles son algunos de los premios que ha ganado Ozuna?

5. ¿Qué está haciendo Ozuna para ayudar a los niños?

Actividad

Ozuna comenzó su colección de relojes porque él recibió un reloj que le regaló su abuela. ¿Coleccionas algo? Si es así, ¿qué coleccionas? Si no, ¿qué te gustaría coleccionar? Dibuja o escribe acerca de los artículos que están o estarían en tu colección. ¿Cuántos te gustaría tener? ¿Cuál es tu parte favorita de tu colección? ¿Cómo cuidarás tu colección y la mantendrás segura? ¿Compartirías tu colección con otras personas?

About the Author
Sobre la autora

Jolene Gutiérrez has one favorite watch and collects interesting rocks and books. She works as a teacher-librarian at a school in Denver, Colorado. Connecting students with books and sharing information are some of Jolene's favorite things. Learn more about Jolene, her writing, and her dreams at www.jolenegutierrez.com.

• • •

Jolene Gutiérrez tiene un reloj favorito y colecciona rocas y libros interesantes. Jolene trabaja como maestra y bibliotecaria en una escuela en Denver, Colorado. Conectar a los estudiantes con libros y compartir información son algunas de las cosas favoritas de Jolene. Obtén más información sobre Jolene, sus escritos y sus sueños en www.jolenegutierrez.com.

www.rourkeeducationalmedia.com

Quote source: Caramanica, Jon. "Reggaeton, Bachata, Latin Trap? Ozuna Does It All." The New York Times. September 3, 2017: https://www.nytimes.com/2017/09/03/arts/music/ozuna-odisea-latin-pop.html ; Lowe, Laurence. "Ozuna In Puerto Rico Interview: A Latin Superstar's Homecoming." Billboard. February 15, 2018: https://www.billboard.com/articles/columns/latin/8099697/ozuna-interview-puerto-rico-latin-superstar-homecoming. ; Reichard, Raquel. "Ozuna is on the Brink of Global Superstardom." The FADER. October 4, 2017: https://www.thefader.com/2017/10/04/ozuna-interview-odisea-tu-foto-se-preparo ; Schiller, Rebecca. "Ozuna Video Interview: Latin Star Talks Odisea Children Charity." Billboard. February 16, 2018 ; https://www.billboard.com/articles/columns/latin/8112052/ozuna-charity-odisea-children-interview.

PHOTO CREDITS: Cover: ©Alberto E. Tamargo/Sipa USA / Newscom; page 3: ©Alberto E. Tamargo/Sipa USA / Newscom (top); page 3: ©JC Olivera/Sipa US / Newscom (bottom); page 5: ©Sean Pavone / Shutterstock; page 5: ©ArnaPhoto / Shutterstock; page 7: ©Mariano Montella / Shutterstock; page 8: ©Johnny Louis/JL/Sipa USA / Newscom; page 9: ©Alberto E. Tamargo/Sipa USA / Newscom; page 13: ©JAVIER ROJAS/EFE / Newscom; page 15: ©JIM RUYMEN/UPI / Newscom; page 16: ©B2820/Retna/Avalon.red / Newscom; page 17: ©Joseph Marzullo/WENN.com / Newscom; page 18: ©GARY I ROTHSTEIN/UPI/ / Newscom; page 19: ©Alberto E. Tamargo/Sipa USA / Newscom; page 20: ©Alberto E. Tamargo/Sipa USA / Newscom; page 21: ©Astrida / SplashNews / Newscom; page 22: ©Orlando Barría/EFE / Newscom; page 23: ©JIM RUYMEN/UPI / Newscom; page 25: ©Juanmonino / Getty Images; page 27: ©JEAN-FRANCOIS Manuel / Shutterstock; page 29: ©Alberto E. Tamargo/Sipa USA / Newscom(top)

Library of Congress PCN Data

Ozuna / Jolene Gutiérrez
(Stars of Latin Pop)
ISBN 978-1-73164-336-0 (hard cover)
ISBN 978-1-73164-300-1 (soft cover)
ISBN 978-1-73164-368-1 (e-Book)
ISBN 978-1-73164-400-8 (ePub)
Library of Congress Control Number: 2020945089

Rourke Educational Media
Printed in the United States of America
01-3502011937

Edited by: Madison Capitano
Cover design by: Michelle Rutschilling
Interior design by: Book Buddy Media